BEAUTIFUL
Birds

More than 900 bird species are found in southern Africa, of which more than 125 occur nowhere else in the world. A kaleidoscope of colour and form, these range from the tiny iridescent sunbirds to the Ostrich, the world's largest living bird.
Above: *Little Bee-eaters;* Right: *Southern Crowned Crane;*
Far right: *Yellowbilled Egret.*

Es existieren über 900 Vogelarten im südlichen Afrika, von denen 125 Arten nur auf dem afrikanischen Kontinent an-zutreffen sind. Es ist ein Kaleidoskop an Farben und Formen, welches vom kleinen, schillernden Nektarvogel bis zum Vogel Strauß reicht, dem größten lebenden Vogel auf dieser Welt.
Oben: *Zwergspint;* Rechts: *Kronenkranich;*
Ganz rechts: *Edelreiher*

L'Afrique australe compte plus de 900 espèces d'oiseaux, dont 125 n'existent nulle part ailleurs dans le monde. Véritable kaléidoscope de couleurs et de formes, on trouve dans cette région tout aussi bien le minuscule souïmanga, au plumage irisé, que l'autruche, le plus grand oiseau vivant du monde.
En haut: *Guêpiers nains;* A droite: *Grue royale;*
Ci-contre à droite: *Aigrette intermédiare.*

🇬🇧 *Stately and elegant, cranes are well known for their graceful dancing displays and far-carrying calls. The Blue Crane (above) is South Africa's national bird. The Southern Crowned Crane (far right) is believed by the Xhosa people to be a harbinger of rain. All cranes are sensitive to disturbance while breeding; this has possibly contributed to recent decreases in the population of the Wattled Crane (right).*

🇩🇪 *Kraniche: Die eleganten Bewohner der Sumpfgebiete und Graseebenen sind bekannt für ihre weittragenden Rufe und graziösen Tanzvorführungen. Der Paradiskranich (oben) ist der Nationalvogel Südafrikas, der Kronenkranich (ganz rechts) wird von den Xhosa verehrt, da diese meinen, der Vogel bringe Regen. Kraniche reagieren empfindlich, wenn sie beim Brüten gestört werden; man sieht darin eine Ursache für den Populationsrückgang derKlunkerkraniche (rechts).*

🇫🇷 *Majestueux habitants des marais, les grues sont réputées pour les sons bruyants qu'elles émettent ainsi que pour leurs parades élégantes. La grue de paradis (ci-dessus) est l'oiseau national d'Afrique du Sud et la grue royale (ci-contre à droite) est un oiseau protégé par les Xhosas parce que, selon eux , il annonce la pluie. Très sensibles à l'époque de la reproduction, les grues ne doivent pas être dérangées et l'on pense que c'est ce facteur qui explique en grande partie la diminution, ces dernières années, du nombre des grues caronculées (à droite).*

Awe-inspiring and powerful, the large birds of prey are truly the kings of the African skies. Although some of the larger eagles, such as the Martial Eagle (left), hunt and capture prey up to the size of a small antelope, other big birds of prey, including the distinctive and brightly coloured Bateleur (above), rely largely or exclusively on scavenging at carcasses or road kills which they locate from the air in effortless, gliding flight.

Große Raubvögel: Die furchteinflößenden und kraftvollen Raubvögel sind die wahren Könige der Lüfte. Während einige der großen Adler, wie beispielsweise der Kampfadler (links), Wild bis zur Größe einer Antilope jagen und erlegen, ernähren sich andere Raubvögel wie der farbige Gaukler (oben) hauptsächlich oder ausschließlich von Aas, das sie von hoch oben aus der Luft erspähen, während sie mühelos durch die Wolken dahingleiten.

Impressionnants et puissants, les grands oiseaux de proie sont incontestablement les rois du ciel africain. Bien que parmi les grands aigles, certains, comme l'aigle martial (à gauche), chassent et capturent des proies qui peuvent atteindre la taille d'une jeune antilope, d'autres par contre, y compris l'aigle bateleur aux vives couleurs (ci-dessus), se contentent de se nourrir de charognes qu'ils décèlent aisément du haut du ciel lors de leurs évolutions à haute altitude.

The Lammergeier (above) is one of the last vultures to feed at a carcass. It has the unusual habit of dropping bones from great heights in order to smash them open, and then swallowing the pieces. The stately Black Eagle (right), by contrast, actively hunts its main prey items, rock hyraxes (or dassies), along the edges of cliffs.

Große Raubvögel: Der Lämmergeier (oben) ist einer der letzten Geier, die sich mit Aas abgeben. Er hat die ungewöhnliche Angewohnheit, die Knochen aus großer Höhe fallen zu lassen, um sie zu zerschmettern und dann verschlingen zu können. Der würdevolle Felsenadler (rechts) jagt hingegen Klippschliefer die Felsen entlang. Manchmal jagen diese Vögel auch paarweise: Der arglose Klippschliefer schaut noch dem ersten Adler nach, der davonfliegt, während er vom zweiten Partner, der von hinten kommt, erlegt wird.

Le gypaète barbu (ci-dessus), qui se contente des derniers restes, est l'un des derniers vautours à festoyer sur les charognes. Du haut des airs, il laisse tomber les os sur les rochers où ils se brisent en menus fragments et dont il se nourrit. En revanche, le majestueux aigle de Verreaux (à droite) chasse les damans des rochers aux abords des falaises. Il lui arrive de chasser en couple et lorsque le daman imprudemment pointe son museau après le passage du premier aigle, le deuxième compère en profite alors pour le capturer.

Lacking the size and power of the great eagles, smaller hawks and falcons rely on speed and agility to catch their fast-moving prey. The rounded wings of the hawks, such as the African Goshawk (left) and the Ovambo Sparrowhawk (above) provide exceptional manœuvrability in woodland and forest when pursuing small birds. The longer wings of the Greater Kestrel (right) allow it to hover in search of small ground-dwelling prey.

Kleine Raubvögel: Da sie die Kraft und Größe der Adler nicht besitzen, sind die kleineren Falken und Habichte besonders flink und agil, um ihr schnell-bewegliches Wild fangen zu können. Die runden Schwingen der Habichte, wie die des Afrikanischen Sperbers (links) und des Ovambosperbers (oben), weisen eine unglaubliche Manövrierfähigkeit in Wäldern auf, wenn sie kleine Vögel ver-folgen. Die langen Flügel des Rötelfalken (rechts) erlauben ihm, auf der Suche nach kleiner, am Boden lebender Beute, schwebend Ausschau zu halten.

Bien qu'ils n'aient pas la taille et la puissance des grands aigles, les éper-viers et les faucons comptent sur leur vitesse et leur agilité pour attraper leur proie. L'arrondi des ailes des éperviers, chez l'autour tachiro (à gauche) et l'éper-vier de l'Ovambo (ci-dessus) par exemple, leur permettent de manoeuvrer avec une extrême efficacité dans les bois et les forêts quand ils s'attaquent aux oiseaux de petite taille. Les ailes plus longues du crécerelle aux yeux blancs (à droite) lui permettent de planer lorsqu'il est en quête de petites proies terrestres.

In the Middle East and north Africa bustards have been hunted to the edge of extinction by high-society falconers. By contrast, southern Africa has a rich diversity of bustards; half of the world's bustard species are found here and many, such as the Redcrested Korhaan (right) and the Northern Black Korhaan (far right), are common and widespread. The Blackbellied Korhaan (above) is a bird of the eastern and northern savannas. The imposing Kori Bustard (top right) is one of the largest flying birds on earth.

Trappen: Im Mittleren Osten und in Nordafrika sind Trappen fast bis zu ihrer Ausrottung von Falknern gejagt worden. Südafrika hingegen besitzt eine reiche Vielfalt an Trappen, die Hälfte der Arten kann man dort finden, und viele Vögel, wie z.B. die Rotschopftrappe (rechts) und die Gakkeltrappe (ganz rechts), sind weit verbreitet. Die Schwarzbauchtrappe (oben) ist ein Vogel der östlichen und nördlichen Savanne. Die beeindruckende Riesentrappe (oben rechts) ist einer der größten fliegenden Vögel auf dieser Erde.

Au Moyen Orient et en Afrique du Nord, les busards ont pratiquement disparu, suite à la pratique de la fauconnerie. En revanche, l'Afrique du Sud compte une grande diversité de busards et on y trouve la moitié de la totalité des espèces existant au monde. Certaines d'entre elles, comme l'outarde houpette (à droite) et l'outarde korhaan du nord (ci-contre à droite), sont très répandues. L'outarde à ventre noir (ci-dessus) habite les régions de savane du nord et de l'est. L'outarde kori (en haut à droite) est l'un des plus grands oiseaux volants du monde.

A stealthy, high-stepping gait typifies the hunting behaviour of both the Yellowbilled Egret (above) and the Yellowbilled Stork (left). *The latter is confined largely to the tropical and subtropical areas of the east and north, whereas the former is widespread throughout the moister regions of southern Africa.*

Fischfresser: Eine würdevolle, weitausschreitende Gangart ist typisch für den Edelreiher (oben) und den Nimmersatt (links). Letzterer ist hauptsächlich in den tropischen und subtropischen Gegenden des Ostens und Nordens anzutreffen, ersterer hat sich über die feuchten Regionen des südlichen Afrika ausgebreitet.

Quand elles chassent, l'aigrette intermédiaire (ci-dessus), tout comme le tantale africain (à gauche) déplient de façon caractéristique leurs longues pattes et se déplacent à pas feutrés. Cette dernière habite surtout les régions tropicales et subtropicales de l'est et du nord, alors que l'aigrette intermédiaire est largement répandue dans toute l'Afrique australe dans les régions les plus humides.

Fish-eating birds come in many sizes, shapes and colours, each with its own solution for tackling slippery prey. Both the African Fish Eagle (below) and the Saddlebilled Stork (right) prey on large fish; in the case of the eagle these may weigh three kilograms or more. The fish eagle captures its prey in its talons after a swooping downward glide, whereas the stork stands and waits for unwary fish to come within range of its stabbing bill.

Fischfresser: Fischfressende Vögel gibt es in vielfacher Form, Farbe und Ausprägung, eine jede Art mit ihrer individuellen Methode, die schlüpfrige Beute zu fangen. Der Schreiseeadler (unten) und der Sattelstorch (rechts) jagen große Fische; die Beute des Adlers kann drei Kilogramm und mehr wiegen. Der Schreiseeadler fängt seine Beute mit seinen Fängen, indem er nach unten stürtzt, während der Storch stehend auf unaufmerksame Fische wartet, die in den Bereich seines langen Schnabels schwimmen.

Les oiseaux qui se nourrissent de poissons varient en tailles, en formes et en couleurs, et chacun use d'un stratagème bien particulier pour traquer sa proie frétillante. L'aigle pêcheur (ci-dessous) tout comme le jabiru d'Afrique (à droite) s'attaquent à de gros poissons qui dans le cas de l'aigle pêcheur peuvent peser plus de trois kilos. Rapide comme l'éclair, l'aigle pêcheur fond sur sa proie et la saisit dans ses serres alors que le jabiru d'Afrique attend patiemment qu'un poisson imprudent vienne à la portée de son bec effilé.

🇬🇧 *Many of the smaller waterbirds do not have powerful talons or long, stork-like legs. They must therefore catch their prey by swimming, as do Darters (far right), and by diving, as does the Giant Kingfisher (right). The African Skimmer (above) has a unique fishing technique: the lower mandible is longer than the upper and is used to 'trawl' through the water, snapping shut automatically when a fish is located.*

Fischfresser: Viele kleinere Wasservögel haben keine kraftvollen Krallen oder lange, storchenähnliche Beine. Sie müssen ihre Beute deshalb schwimmend fangen, wie es die Schlangenhalsvögel (ganz rechts) tun, oder tauchen, so wie der Rieseneisvogel (rechts). Der Braunmantel-Scherenschnabel (oben) hat eine einzigartige Fischtechnik: Der untere Kiefer ist länger als der obere und wird wie ein Netz benutzt. Ist ein Fisch "im Netz", schließt sich der Schnabel, die Beute ist in der Falle.

🇫🇷 *Bien des oiseaux aquatiques de plus petite taille ne possèdent pas de serres puissantes ou de longues pattes. Ils doivent alors capturer leur proie à la nage, comme ces anhingas d'Afrique (ci-contre à droite), ou en plongeant comme c'est le cas pour ce martin-pêcheur géant (à droite). Le bec-en-ciseaux d'Afrique (ci-dessus) possède une manière unique de pêcher: sa mandibule inférieure, plus longue que sa mandibule supérieure, lui permet d' 'écumer' la surface de l'eau. Lorsqu'il aperçoit un poisson, son bec se referme automatiquement sur sa proie.*

An abundance of small herons is a characteristic feature of Africa's wetlands. Many species, including the Squacco Heron (below), a solitary and skulking bird, hunt in shallow waters. Little Egrets (bottom left) are much more energetic hunters and can often be seen running frantically to and fro, making dart-like stabs at shoals of small fish. The Black Egret (left) displays a unique hunting behaviour in which it opens its wings forwards to form a complete umbrella, with its head pointing down in the middle. It may do this to fool the fish that shelter is at hand when danger threatens from above; little do the fish know that they have been caught in a perfect trap.

Kleine Reiher: Eine Ansammlung kleiner Reiher ist ein typischer Anblick in den Feuchtgebieten Afrikas. Viele Arten, einschließlich des Rallenreihers (unten), jagen im flachen Wasser. Seidenreiher (unten links) sind sehr energiegeladene Jäger, die man häufig hin und her laufen sehen kann, wobei sie im Wasser nach kleinen Fischen und Schwärmen picken. Der Glockenreiher (links) hat eine einzigartige Jagdweise: Er öffnet seine Flügel wie einen Regenschirm, den Kopf mittig nach unten gebeugt. Wahrscheinlich tut er dies, um die Fische von der eigentlichen Gefahr, seinem Schnabel abzulenken.

Les régions marécageuses d'Afrique se caractérisent par une grande quantité de petits hérons. Bien des espèces, y compris le héron crabier (ci-dessous), chassent dans les eaux peu profondes. Les aigrettes garzettes (ci-dessous à gauche) sont des chasseurs intrépides et on peut souvent les apercevoir arpentant de long en large les rives et piquant, ici et là, de petits poissons avec leur long bec effilé. L'aigrette ardoisée (à gauche) a une façon unique de chasser: elle déploie ses ailes devant elle comme un parapluie qui recouvre complètement son corps à l'exception de sa tête baissée.

Although most fish-eating birds hunt by day, a few emerge to hunt only in the darkness of the night. These catch prey by stealth, from the silent downward plunge of Pel's Fishing Owl (right) to the measured, slow stalk of the Blackcrowned Night Heron (left) and Whitebacked Night Heron (below). By confining their hunting to the hours of darkness, these birds avoid competing with the many species of herons, kingfishers and other fish-eaters that patrol Africa's waterways, lakes and pans during daylight.

Nächtliche Fischfresser: Obwohl die meisten fischfressenden Vögel am Tag auf Beutefang gehen, gibt es einige, die nur in der Dunkelheit der Nacht jagen. Es sind die heimlichen Jäger wie die leise tauchende Fischeule (rechts) oder der abschätzende, langsam einherschreitende Nachtreiher (links) und der Weißrücken-Nachtreiher (unten). Dadurch, daß diese Tiere in der Nacht jagen, vermeiden sie den Wettbewerb mit vielen anderen Reiherarten wie dem Eisvogel und anderen Vögeln, die tagsüber an den Wasserwegen und Pfannen Afrikas patrouillieren.

Bien que la plupart des oiseaux qui se nourrissent de poissons chassent pendant la journée, certains sortent pour chasser uniquement à la tombée de la nuit. Ce sont des chasseurs furtifs qui, comme le chouette-pêcheuse de Pel (à droite), plongent silencieusement dans l'eau, ou qui, comme le héron bihoreau (à gauche) et le bihoreau à dos blanc (ci-dessous), d'un long pas mesuré guettent leur proie. Ces chasseurs nocturnes évitent ainsi la concurrence des nombreuses autres espèces de hérons et de martins-pêcheurs qui patrouillent étangs et marais pendant la journée.

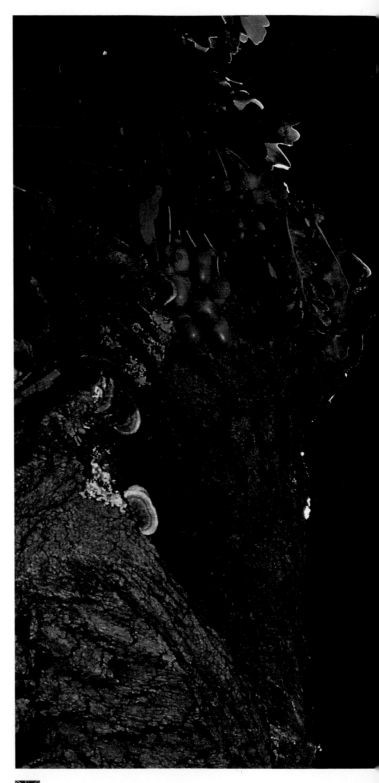

The large, rounded eyes of owls are modified to provide them with excellent night vision. However, most of the birds' prey also see well at night, and much of an owl's success as a hunter is dependent on a silent attack. Their ghost-like flight is rendered noiseless by specially modified flight feathers. A few owls are active by day, but most, such as the Spotted Eagle Owl (top left and left), pass the daylight hours resting quietly in trees or among rocks. The Barn Owl (above and right) is closely associated with man, nesting and roosting in roofs and outbuildings. It performs a valuable service in catching mice and other rodents.

Eulen: Die großen, runden Augen der Eulen sind besonders gut entwickelt, um in der Nacht zu sehen. Allerdings sieht der Großteil ihrer Beutetiere auch gut in der Nacht, und der Jagderfolg einer Eule hängt sehr davon ab, wie leise sie angreift. Durch eine besondere Modifizierung ihrer Flügel fliegen die Eulen lautlos. Einige Eulen sind tagsüber wach, aber die meisten, wie z. B. der Berguhu (unten links und links) verbringen den Tag, indem sie in Bäumen ruhen. Die Schleiereule (oben und rechts) ist dem Menschen sehr verbunden, sie nistet auf Dächern und Gebäuden. Sie ist außergewöhnlich gut im Mäusefangen.

Les hiboux ont de grands yeux ronds qui sont adaptés à la vision nocturne. Toutefois, leurs proies voient également bien la nuit et, pour que la chasse soit fructueuse, le hibou doit compter sur le silence de son approche. Ses ailes, spécialement conçues pour ne pas faire de bruit, lui permettent de voler comme un fantôme. Certains hiboux sont actifs pendant la journée mais, la plupart d'entre eux, comme le grand-duc africain (en haut à gauche et à gauche), passent le plus clair de leur temps à se reposer. La chouette effraie (ci-dessus et à droite) aime les lieux habités par l'homme et s'installe volontiers sous les toits des maisons.

The Helmeted Guineafowl (above) is one of southern Africa's best known and most conspicuous gamebirds. Groups of these noisy and comical birds are often encountered along roads during the day; at night they roost in groups in trees. Burchell's Sandgrouse (left) are found in the Kalahari Desert. Despite their desert existence, these birds drink daily – always in the morning – gathering in flocks at waterholes. Drinking flocks are constantly alert to the danger posed by hawks and falcons which perch close by, on the lookout for an easy meal.

Federwild: Das Helmperlhuhn (oben) ist eines der bekanntesten und auffallendsten Tiere unter dem Federwild. Gruppen dieser lauten und komischen Vögel findet man tagsüber oft entlang der Straßen, nachts schlafen sie in Gruppen auf Bäumen. Das Fleckenflughuhn (links) findet man in der Kalahariwüste. Obwohl sie in der Wüste leben, müssen sie täglich etwas trinken, so sie sammeln sich an Wasserlöchern. Während des Trinkens sind sie sich jederzeit der Gefahren durch Habichte oder Falken bewußt, die in der Nähe umherfliegen und Ausschau nach einer leichten Beute halten.

Parmi le gibier à plumes, la pintade commune (ci-dessus) est l'oiseau le plus répandu en Afrique australe. Pendant la journée, il n'est pas rare de trouver en groupes, aux abords des routes, ces oiseaux bruyants et à l'allure comique; la nuit, ils s'installent dans les arbres. Le ganga de Burchell (à gauche) habite le désert du Kalahari. Bien que ces oiseaux vivent dans le désert, ils ont besoin de boire tous les jours et se rassemblent en colonies aux points d'eau, où ils se tiennent sur le qui-vive à cause des éperviers et des faucons perchés non loin de là dans l'espoir de faire un repas copieux.

Southern Africa is home to 12 species of francolin and four species of sandgrouse. Redbilled Francolins (below), like many other francolin species, eat the bulbs and corms of plants which they dig up with their feet and bills. Sandgrouse, by contrast, eat mostly small seeds which they pick from the soil surface. The Doublebanded Sandgrouse (left), like Burchell's Sandgrouse (opposite, bottom), drinks daily but comes to waterholes only after sunset, having spent much of the day resting in the shade.

Federwild: Das südliche Afrika ist die Heimat von 12 Arten der Frankoline und von vier Arten der Flughühner. Sandhühner (unten) fressen, wie viele ihrer Art, die Knollen der Pflanzen, die sie mit ihren Krallen und Schnäbeln ausgraben. Flughühner fressen im Gegensatz dazu eher kleine Samen, welche sie von der Erde aufpicken. Das Nachtflughuhn (links) und das Fleckenflughuhn (gegenüber) trinken jeden Tag, kommen aber erst nach Sonnenuntergang ans Wasserloch, nachdem sie den größten Teil des Tages im Schatten geruht haben.

On trouve en Afrique australe 12 espèces de francolins et quatre espèces de ganga. Les francolins à bec rouge (ci-dessous), tout comme bien d'autres espèces de francolins, se nourrissent des bulbes des plantes qu'ils déterrent à l'aide de leurs pattes et de leur bec. Le ganga, par contre, consomme essentiellement des petites graines qu'il picore sur le sol. Le ganga bibande (à gauche), comme le ganga de Burchell (ci-contre, en bas), s'abreuvent chaque jour mais ne se rendent aux points d'eau qu'au crépuscule, après avoir passé la journée à se reposer à l'ombre.

Many of the waders that visit the coasts and lakes of southern Africa during the summer have flown more than 12 000 kilometres from their breeding grounds in the Arctic tundras and the taigas of central Siberia. The Ruff (right) comes even further, from breeding grounds close to the Bering Strait. Other waders, such as the Ethiopian Snipe (above) and the Avocet (right, above), live in southern Africa throughout the year, moving around the region in response to seasonal rainfall. The tiny Chestnutbanded Plover (far right) hunts for its food at the edges of very saline pans – a habitat it shares with few other birds.

Stelz- oder Watvögel: Viele der Watvögel, die die Küsten und Seen des südlichen Afrikas im Sommer besuchen, sind über 12 000km von ihren Brutsätten in der Antarktis bis nach Afrika geflogen. Der Kampfläufer (rechts) hat den weitesten Weg, seine Brutstätten liegen nahe der Beringstraße. Andere, wie die Afrikanische Bekassine (oben) und der Säbelschnebler (rechts oben) leben im südlichen Afrika und ziehen jeweils in die Regionen, in denen Regen fällt. Der kleine Fahlregenpfeifer (ganz rechts) ernährt sich an den äußeren Enden der Salzpfannen – eine Eigenart, die er mit nur wenigen anderen Vögeln teilt.

Parmi les échassiers qui migrent sur les côtes et les lacs d'Afrique australe en été, bon nombre d'entre eux viennent des zones de toundra des régions arctiques où ils se reproduisent après avoir parcouru plus de 12 000 kilomètres. Celui qui entreprend la migration la plus lointaine est le chevalier combattant (à droite), car il vient des régions situées à proximité du détroit de Béring, son aire de reproduction. D'autres échassiers comme la bécassine africaine (ci-dessus) et l'avocette à tête noire (à droite, ci-dessus), vivent en Afrique australe toute l'année. Le minuscule pluvier élégant (ci-contre à droite) cherche sa nourriture près des cuvettes de sel.

Dense beds of reeds and mats of floating vegetation are favoured habitats for a suite of birds both large and small. The Glossy Ibis (right) stalks its prey in shallow water at the edges of reedbeds. The reedbeds themselves provide nesting sites for a host of small, noisy and brightly coloured birds, including the Red Bishop (left) and Spottedbacked Weaver (below). Many of these small birds breed in dense colonies, constructing hanging, ball-like nests woven from strips of reeds.

Küstenvögel: Dichtes Schilf und Matten von Wasserpflanzen sind die bevorzugten Habitate für eine Reihe großer und kleiner Vögel. Der Braune Sichler (rechts) erlegt seine Beute im flachen Wasser an den Enden der Schilffelder. Das Schilfrohr selbst bietet einer Anzahl kleinerer, lauter und farbenfroher Vögel Platz zum Nisten. Unter diesen ist der Oryxweber (links) und der Dorfweber (unten). Viele dieser kleinen Vögel brüten in dichten Kolonien; sie bauen hängende, runde Nester, die sie aus Schilf anfertigen.

Les zones de marais couvertes de lits de roseaux et de végétation à fleur d'eau sont l'habitat favori d'une myriade d'oiseaux de toutes tailles. L'ibis falcinelle (à droite) guette sa proie dans les eaux peu profondes au bord des roseaux. Beaucoup de petits oiseaux piailleurs et au vif plumage font leur nid dans les roseaux, comme cet euplecte ignicolore (à gauche) et ce tisserin gendarme (ci-dessous). Plusieurs de ces petits oiseaux se reproduisent dans des colonies denses et construisent des nids faits de brins de roseaux, qu'ils suspendent aux branches des arbres.

Several southern African kingfishers, including the Pied
Kingfisher (left) *and Malachite Kingfisher* (above), *are always
found at or near water. Others, however, both breed and feed
away from water. The Brownhooded Kingfisher* (right) *is one such
species: it preys on large insects and small lizards and is plentiful
in the eastern and northern savannas, extending its range through
the coastal lowlands to the southwestern Cape.*

*Eisvögel: Einige südafrikanische Eisvögel, wie der Grau-
fischer* (links) *und der Malachiteisvogel* (oben), *findet man immer
in Wassernähe. Andere wiederum brüten und leben fern vom
Wasser. Der Braunkopfliest* (rechts) *ist einer davon: Er jagt
kleine Eidechsen und große Insekten in den östlichen und nördlichen Savannen, und ist vom Küstenflachland bis zum südwest-
lichen Kap anzutreffen.*

*En Afrique australe plusieurs espèces de martins-pêcheurs
habitent dans le voisinage immédiat de l'eau, comme c'est le cas
pour le martin-pêcheur pie* (à gauche) *et le martin-pêcheur huppé*
(ci-dessus). *D'autres, en revanche, se reproduisent et se nourrissent loin de l'eau, comme le martin-chasseur à tête brune* (à
droite) *qui s'attaque aux grands insectes et aux petits lézards; il
est très répandu dans les régions de savane du nord et de l'est et
son aire de répartition s'étend des basses terres du littoral jusqu' à
la région du Cap du sud-ouest.*

Southern Africa is home to no fewer than 14 species of pigeon and dove. Several of these, including the strikingly coloured Green Pigeon (below) and the Rameron Pigeon (bottom left), are commonly found in towns and cities. Here they gather in flocks to gorge themselves on fruits, especially figs. Other species, including the Tambourine Dove (right) and Bluespotted Dove (left), are much shyer birds, usually encountered only fleetingly in dense woodland and forest.

Tauben: Das südliche Afrika ist die Heimat von ungefähr 14 Taubenarten. Die farbenfrohe Grüntaube (unten) und die Oliventaube (ganz unten links) trifft man meist in Städten an. Dort versammeln sie sich, um am Obst zu picken, wovon sie Feigen bevorzugen. Andere Taubenarten wie die Tamburintaube (rechts) und die Stahlfleckentaube (links) sind scheuere Vögel, die man häufig in Wäldern und dicht bewaldeten Gegenden antrifft.

On compte en Afrique australe pas moins de 14 espèces de colombes et de pigeons, et bon nombre de ces oiseaux vivent dans les villes et les agglomérations. Comme c'est le cas pour le pigeon vert (ci-dessous) et le pigeon rameron (en bas à gauche), deux oiseaux aux couleurs frappantes. Ici, ils se rassemblent en colonies pour se gaver de fruits et en particulier de figues. D'autres espèces, comme la tourtelette tambourette (à droite) et l'emerauldine à bec rouge (à gauche) sont beaucoup plus craintives et on ne les aperçoit habituellement que d'une manière fugace dans les régions densément boisées et dans les forêts.

🇬🇧 *Swooping and diving, often in large flocks, their bright colours electric in the African sun, bee-eaters are among the most beautiful of the region's birds. Most of the species, including the Whitefronted (right), Little (left) and Swallowtailed (above) bee-eaters, have tropical and subtropical distributions. They hunt their insect prey on the wing, and make their nests – almost always in colonies – in holes dug in the sides of sandbanks. Carmine Bee-eaters (above left) sometimes ride on the backs of Kori Bustards, using the bustards as 'beaters' to disturb insects.*

▬ *Bienenfresser: Sie gleiten durch die Luft und stoßen plötz-lich herab, meist zu mehreren. Mit ihren strahlenden Farben gehö-ren die Bienenfresser zu den schönsten Vögeln unter der Sonne Südafrikas. Die meisten dieser Spezie, wie z.B. der Weißstirnspint (rechts) und der Zwergspint (links) sowie der Gabelschwanzspint (oben), kann man in tropisch oder subtropisch einteilen. Sie jagen Insekten und bauen ihre Nester, meist als Kolonien, in Löcher, die sie in Sandbänke graben. Der Scharlachspint (oben links) reitet manchmal auf dem Rücken einer Riesentrappe mit, und benutzt ihn als Treiber, um die Insekten aufzustöbern.*

🇫🇷 *Les guêpiers, qui souvent en bandes fondent sur leurs proies sous le soleil africain, font vibrer l'air de leurs couleurs écla-tantes aux reflets irisés. C'est l'une des plus belles espèces d'oiseaux de la région. La plupart d'entre eux, comme le guêpier à front blanc (à droite), le guêpier nain (à gauche) et le guêpier à queue d'hirondelle (ci-dessus) habitent les régions tropicales et subtropicales. Ils chassent les insectes en plein vol et font leur nid dans des trous creusés le long des bancs de sable. Le guêpier carmin (ci-dessus à gauche) grimpe parfois sur le dos des busards de kori afin de 'rabattre' les insectes.*

Rollers are the jewels of the African savannas. Resplendent in shades and sheens of blue, turquoise and violet, they never cease to amaze and delight the traveller. During the summer months, European Rollers (below) migrate south to join the resident Lilacbreasted Rollers (left). In well-wooded areas, the uncommon and surprisingly inconspicuous Racket-tailed Roller (bottom) may be found resting quietly just below the canopy of a tree.

Flugtauben: Tümmlertauben sind die Juwelen der afrikanischen Savanne. Sie begeistern und erfreuen mit ihren schillernden Blautönen, ihrem Türkis und Lila einen jeden Reisenden. Im Sommer fliegt die Blauracke (unten) nach Süden, um die Gabelracke (links) zu besuchen. In schönen, waldigen Gebieten trifft man auf die seltene und ungewöhnliche Spatelracke (ganz unten), die man friedlich ruhend unter einen Blätterdach antreffen kann.

Les rolliers sont les fleurons de la savane africaine. Avec leur plumage lustré aux couleurs chatoyantes, ils ne cessent d'étonner et de réjouir le voyageur. Pendant les mois d'été, les rolliers d'Europe (ci-dessous) migrent en direction du sud pour se joindre aux rolliers à longs brins (à gauche), qui, eux, sont sédentaires. Dans les régions boisées, il arrive qu'on puisse voir, paisiblement à l'abri sous un arbre, le rollier à raquettes (en bas), oiseau rare qui passe souvent inaperçu.

The delicate, curved bills of the sunbirds and Cape Sugarbird (below) are special adaptations which enable them to probe deeply into flowers to obtain energy-rich nectar. In exchange for their sweet meal, these birds play an important role in pollinating flowers. Some plants, especially heathers, have strengthened stems which allow the Orangebreasted Sunbird (right) and Lesser Doublecollared Sunbird (far right) to perch easily. Unlike the hummingbirds of the New World, sunbirds and sugarbirds do not habitually hover while feeding.

Nektarvögel: Der kunstvoll geformte Bauch des südafrikanischen Nektarvogels hat eine besondere Form, die es dem Vogel ermöglicht, tief in die Blume einzudringen, um an den Nektar zu gelangen. Im Austausch für dieses süße Mahl sind die Vögel wichtig für die Bestäubung der Blumen. Einige Pflanzen, und besonders das Heidekraut, haben einen sehr starken Stengel, was es dem Goldbrustnektarvogel (rechts) und dem Halsband-Nektarvogel (ganz rechts) erleichtert, darauf zu sitzen. Im Gegensatz zum südamerikanischen Kolibri schweben Nektarvögel und Honigfresser normalerweise nicht, wenn sie die Jungen füttern.

Le bec délicatement recourbé des souïmangas et des promerops du Cap (ci-dessous) est conçu tout spécialement pour pouvoir puiser le riche nectar au coeur des fleurs. En échange de ces délices, ces oiseaux jouent un rôle important dans la pollinisation des fleurs. Certaines plantes, les bruyères en particulier, ont des tiges rigides qui permettent aux souïmangas orange (à droite) et aux souïmangas chalybées (ci-contre à droite) de se percher facilement. Contrairement à l'oiseau-mouche du Nouveau Monde, les souïmangas et les promerops ne voltigent généralement pas au-dessus des plantes quand ils s'alimentent.

Garrulous and bold, many of southern Africa's starlings, including Burchell's Starling (below), have an iridescent sheen to their plumage, reflecting in shades of blue, green and violet. These glossy starlings are common residents of forests and savannas. The Palewinged Starling (bottom left), by contrast, is a bird of dry cliffs and gorges. The Wattled Starling (left) is found throughout the region but is most common in the arid west. Male birds develop black and yellow facial markings during the breeding season.

Stare: Die meisten Stare des südlichen Afrikas, unter ihnen der Riesenglanzstar (unten), sind geschwätzig und frech, ihre Federn haben einen schillernden Schimmer – in Blautönen, in Grün und Violett. Diese schimmernden Stare sind bekannte Bewohner der Wälder und Savannen. Der Bergstar (unten links) hingegen ist ein Vogel der rauhen Klippen und Täler. Der Lappenstar (links) brütet in Kolonien: Während der Brunstzeit bekommen die Männchen schwarze und gelbe Muster im Gesicht.

Babillards et effrontés, la plupart des sansonnets d'Afrique australe, y compris le merle métallique de Burchell (ci-dessous), ont un plumage lustré aux reflets bleus, verts et violets. Ces étourneaux lustrés sont très répandus dans la forêt et la savane. L'étourneau à ailes pâles (en bas à gauche), habite en revanche dans les régions de falaises et de gorges. L'étourneau caronculé (à gauche) niche en colonies: pendant la saison de reproduction, la face des mâles s'orne de motifs noirs et jaunes.

In natural habitats the Redwinged Starling (below) is a bird of mountains and cliffs. The ledges and creeper-covered walls of city buildings, however, provide excellent nest sites for this bird and it is common in many urban areas, where it is often seen pecking dead insects from the bodywork of cars.

In natürlicher Umgebung ist der Rotschwingenstar (unten) ein Vogel der Berge und Klippen. Hauswände bieten dem Vogel in der Stadt eine hervorragende Nistmöglichkeit. So ist er auch in vielen Regionen ein typischer Stadtvogel, der oft die toten Insekten von den Autos aufsammelt.

Dans son habitat naturel, l'étourneau morio (ci-dessous) vit dans les montagnes et les falaises. Toutefois, les murs recouverts de verdure des immeubles lui offrent d'excellents coins pour construire son nid; c'est un oiseau que l'on voit souvent en ville, picorant les insectes écrasés sur les voitures.

The sturdy, hooked bills and sharp, curved claws of the shrikes are well suited to their predatory lifestyles. These birds – many of which, such as the Orangebreasted Bush Shrike (below), are brightly coloured – are active hunters of large insects, reptiles and even birds. Small prey items are sometimes impaled on thorns or spikes before being eaten. Their diet overlaps substantially with that of some of the smaller birds of prey. The Bokmakierie (left) is common and widespread in the southern and western parts of the region, where its ringing call is a characteristic sound of the veld.

Buschwürger: Der robuste und krumme Schnabel sowie die scharfen, gekrümmten Klauen der Buschwürger passen gut zu ihrem räuberischen Lebensstil. Diese Vögel – viele von ihnen, wie der Orangenwürger (unten), sind farbenfroh – sind aktive Jäger größerer Insekten, Reptilien und und sogar Vögel. Kleinere Beutetiere werden manchmal auf Dornen aufgespießt, bevor sie gefressen werden. Die Nahrung dieser Vögel überschneidet sich mit der anderer kleinerer Raubvögel. Der Bokmariki (links) ist weitverbreitet in den südlichen und westlichen Regionen, wo sein klingender Ruf ein typisches Geräusch des Veldes ist.

Les pies-grièches sont munies d'un bec courbé et robuste et de griffes recourbées, parfaitement adaptés à leur style de vie. Ces oiseaux prédateurs chassent de gros insectes, des reptiles et parfois même des oiseaux. La plupart d'entre eux, comme ce gladiateur soufré (ci-dessous), ont de vives couleurs. Ils leur arrivent d'empaler de petites proies sur des épines avant de les avaler. Leur régime alimentaire est pratiquement le même que celui des petits rapaces. Le gladiateur bacbakiri (à gauche) est très répandu dans les parties sud et ouest de la région et son cri aigu est un son caractéristique du veld.

Hole-nesters

Many species of forest and woodland birds nest in holes in trees. Some of these, such as woodpeckers and barbets, are sufficiently strong to excavate their own holes, while others, such as the Hoopoe (above) and the Redthroated Wryneck (top right), have to rely on natural cavities, or take over the abandoned nests of other hole-nesting species. The entrance holes to these nests are as small as possible, so as to keep predators at bay. Hornbills carry this to extremes – for example, once the female Redbilled Hornbill has entered the nest chamber, the entrance is sealed with mud, leaving only a small slit through which the male bird (right) passes food. The female is fed throughout the incubation period and leaves the nest only when the young are half-grown.

Viele Arten der Wald- und Wiesenvögel nisten in Baumlöchern oder Aushöhlungen in Bäumen. Vögel wie der Specht und der Bartvogel sind so stark, daß sie ihre Löcher selbst aushämmern können, während andere Vögel hingegen – wie der Wiedehopf (oben) und der Rotkehl-Wendehals (oben rechts) – auf die Vorgaben der Natur zurückgreifen oder verlassene Nester übernehmen müssen. Die Eingangslöcher dieser Nester sind so klein wie möglich, um Räuber auszuschließen. Die Toko erweitern diese Sichertsmaßnahme: Hat der weibliche Rotschnabeltoko einmal das Nest betreten, so wird der Eingang bis auf ein kleines Loch mit Lehm versiegelt, duch das das Männchen (rechts) das Essen reichen kann, Feinde aber nicht hindurchkommen.

De nombreuses espèces d'oiseaux, qui habitent les régions boisées, nichent dans des trous creusés dans les troncs ou les branches des arbres. Il y a ceux qui creusent leur propre trou, comme les pics-verts et les barbicans, et il y a ceux qui, telle la huppe fasciée (ci-dessus) et le tourcol à gorge rousse (en haut à droite), se contentent de nicher dans des cavités naturelles toutes faites ou dans les nids abandonnés par d'autres espèces d'oiseaux. L'entrée de ces nids est aussi étroite que possible afin d'en empêcher l'accès aux prédateurs. Les calaos sont passés maîtres en ce domaine car, une fois que la femelle du petit calao à bec rouge est entrée dans le nid, l'accès en est bouché par de la boue et seule une étroite fente demeure permettant au mâle (à droite) de faire passer la nourriture.

🇬🇧 *Waxbills are found in a wide range of habitats. The Violeteared Waxbill (left) and Blackcheeked Waxbill (below) extend their ranges into semi-desert habitats, whereas the smaller Swee Waxbill (right) forages among rank, tangled vegetation at forest edges. Early in the breeding season waxbills are often attended by whydahs. The whydahs are parasitic, laying their eggs in waxbill nests and then leaving the waxbills to raise their foster chicks.*

🇩🇪 *Schönbürzel/ Astrilde: Diese Vögel werden in einer großen Anzahl von Habitaten angetroffen. Das Blaubäckchen (links) und der Elfenastrild (unten) sind bis in die Halbwüste verbreitet, wohingegen der Gelbbauchastrild (rechts) sich in einer dichtbewachsenen, dornigen Vegetation in waldnahen Gebieten aufhält. Zu Beginn der Brütezeit werden die Schönbürzel von den Witwen heimgesucht. Letztere sind Parasiten, die ihre Eier in die Nester der ersteren legen und es den Schönbürzel überlassen, die fremden Küken aufzuziehen.*

🇫🇷 *Les astrilds habitent une grande diversité d'habitats. Le cordon bleu à joues violettes (à gauche) et l'astrild à face noire (ci-dessous) ont une aire de répartition qui comprend les régions semi-désertiques, alors que l'astrild à ventre jaune (à droite) fourrage dans taillis et broussailles aux abords des forêts. Au début de la saison de reproduction, les astrilds ont souvent les veuves à leur traîne. La veuve est un oiseau parasite qui pond ses oeufs dans le nid des astrilds et qui ensuite compte sur eux pour élever sa progéniture.*

Flycatchers, as their name implies, eat mainly small flying insects. Most species, including the beautiful Paradise Flycatcher (top) and the Dusky Flycatcher (left), hunt from a perch, where they wait motionless before sallying forth and snapping their prey from the air. The Chinspot Batis (above), common in woodland and savanna, is a much more active hunter, catching its food both in the air and by gleaning insects and spiders from leaves and branches.

Schnäpper: Diese Vögel fressen (schnappen) – wie der Name schon sagt – überwiegend kleine Insekten. Die meisten Arten, wie der wunderbare Paradis-schnäpper (ganz oben) und der Dunkelschnäpper (links), jagen von einem sicheren Sitz aus, auf dem sie bewegungslos warten, bevor sie hervorschießen und ihre Beute schnappen. Der Weißflankenschnäpper (oben) ist ein wesentlich aktiverer Jäger, er fängt seine Beute in der Luft und sammelt Insekten und Spinnen auf Blättern und Ästen ein, die er dann vertilgt. Man trifft sie überwiegend in Waldgebieten und Savannen an.

Comme leur nom l'indique, les gobe-mouches se nourrissènt essentielle-ment de petits insectes. La plupart des espèces, y compris le superbe moucherolle de paradis (en haut) et le gobe-mouche sombre (à gauche), se perchent pour chasser et attendent immobiles le passage de leurs proies qu'elles attrapent alors en plein vol. Le batis molitor (ci-dessus), habitant des régions boisées et de la savane, est un chasseur beaucoup plus actif car non seulement il attrape sa nour-riture en plein vol mais il récolte aussi des insectes et des araignées sur les feuilles et les branches.

The world's largest heron, the Goliath Heron (above), is widely distributed in the tropical and subtropical wetlands of southern Africa. Standing more than one metre high, this powerful predator can spear and swallow fish weighing up to nearly one kilogram.

Der größte Reiher der Welt, der Goliathreiher (oben), ist weit verstreut über die tropischen und subtropischen Feuchtgebiete des südlichen Afrikas. Der Vogel ist über einen Meter groß und ist ein kraftvoller Jäger, der Fisch bis zu einen Kilogramm Gewicht aufspießen und verschlingen kann.

Le héron Goliath (ci-dessus), le héron le plus grand du monde, est très répandu en Afrique australe dans les zones marécageuses des régions tropicales et subtropicales. Haut de plus d'un mètre, ce prédateur puissant est capable de transpercer et d'avaler des poissons pesant près d'un kilogramme.

Struik Publishers (Pty) Ltd (a member of the Struik Publishing Group (Pty) Ltd)
Cornelis Struik House, 80 McKenzie Street
Cape Town 8001
Reg. No.: 54/00965/07

First published 1994

Text © P.A.R. Hockey 1994
Map © Struik Publishers 1994
Photographs © individual photographers and/or their agents as follows:
Anthony Bannister p 2 (top). ABPL/Clem Haagner: p 20 (top), p 41; ABPL/Hein von Hörsten: p 21 (bottom), p 42;
ABPL/Nigel Dennis: p 26 (bottom); ABPL/Daryl Balfour: p 26 (top), p 29 (bottom); ABPL/Tim Liversedge: p 32 (top left);
ABPL/Brendan Ryan: p 32 (top right); ABPL/Richard du Toit: p 34; ABPL/Pat Donaldson: p 35 (top); ABPL/Johan van
Jaarsveld: p 47 (top). J.C. Paterson-Jones: p 4 (top), p 36 (bottom). Nigel Dennis: title page, p 3, p 4 (bottom),
p 6 (top), p 7 (top), p 9 (top), p 10, p 11 (top & bottom left), pp 12-19, p 22 (bottom), p 23 (top), pp 24-25, p 27-28, p 33,
p 43 (bottom), back cover. Roy Johannesson: p 4 (middle); Peter Craig-Cooper: p 2 (bottom), p 6 (bottom), pp 30-31,
p 32 (bottom), p 38, pp 44-45, p 48. May Craig-Cooper: p 20 (bottom), p 23 (bottom), p 39. Colin Urquhart: p 5.
R.M. Bloomfield:p 7(bottom), p 47 (bottom). Hein von Hörsten: p 22 (top), p 36 (top), p 37, p 46. Lanz von Hörsten: cover
(inset, bottom), p 21 (top), p 29 (top), p 40. Claudio Velasquez: p 8. SIL/Peter Pickford: p 9 (bottom). Ian Davidson: p 11
(bottom right). Warwick Tarboton: p 35 (bottom). Alan Weaving: p 43 (top).
© in published edition Struik Publishers 1994

Edited by Pippa Parker
French translation by Cécile Spottiswoode; German translation by Bettina Kaufmann
Designed by Petal Palmer
Map by Lyndall Hamilton
Typesetting by Deirdré Geldenhuys, Struik DTP
Reproduction by Unifoto (Pty) Ltd, Cape Town
Printed and bound by Kyodo Printing Co. (Pte) Ltd

ISBN 1 86825 728 2

Front cover, main photograph *Saddlebilled Stork*, top inset *Malachite Kingfisher*, bottom inset *Paradise Flycatcher*.
Title page *Grey Heron*. Back cover *Lesser Flamingos*.